THE

INTEGRITY

FACTOR

A Journey in Leadership Formation

Kevin W. Mannoia

Library and Archives Canada Cataloguing in Publication

Mannoia, Kevin W.
    The integrity factor : a journey in leadership formation / Kevin W. Mannoia.

Includes bibliographical references.
ISBN 1-57383-349-5

    1. Leadership—Religious aspects—Christianity. 2. Christian leadership.
I. Title.

BV4597.53.L43M355 2006   262'.1   C2006-901913-4

TO KATHLEEN,
MY PARTNER ON THE JOURNEY.

HIDDEN VALLEYS

In a hidden valley just over the hill
A young shepherd boy surrenders his will
As he lifts his voice in praise to his King
Only the lambs will hear and follow as he sings.

In a hidden valley a faithful one leads
No one looking on, he cares for their needs
For he knows the One who tries the heart
So he is steadfast and content to do his part.

Hidden valleys produce a life song
Hidden valleys will make a heart strong
Desperation can cause you to sing
Hidden valleys turn shepherds to kings.

In a hidden valley a leader is born
He has faced the fierce and weathered the storm
So with humble heart and love for his God
He becomes royalty with a staff and rod.

words by Kelly Willard

CONTENTS

FOREWORD

Whatmore can be written on the subject of leadership? For almost three decades now, students of leadership have explored every conceivable factor and produced volumes of books under every conceivable title. Is it the lack of leadership in our basic institutions or the recognition of rare resource that has stimulated this interest? Perhaps it is both. Certainly, a crisis was created in the 1960s when the credibility of legitimate leaders, ranging from national presidents to local clergy, came under fire. In the 1970s, the attacks turned into a self-fulfilling prophecy when Richard Nixon betrayed his presidential trust, taking down with him our confidence in established leaders. Since then, the foibles, flaws and falls of prominent leaders, whether in government, business, education or religion, have repeatedly been exposed by the white-hot glare and penetrating light of the public media. And rightly so. When all is said and done, if character is not the core of leadership after all the layers of charisma, competence, power and position have been peeled away, every theory of leadership – secular or sacred – will have to be revised.

Just the opposite is happening. During the decade of the 1980s and into the 1990s, leadership literature has clearly shifted toward character with integrity as its imprint. One might even go so far as to say that leadership theory is searching for its soul and leadership literature has become a spiritual quest. Slowly, but surely, we have witnessed leadership move from profitable self-interest to value-based service and on to other-directed stewardship. While none of this is Christian, the re-centering of leadership around moral values and people priorities is a giant step toward character as the essential ingredient.

In the midst of this encouraging scene, a sad note must be sounded. At the same time that studies of leadership are accenting character, public opinion is moving in reverse. Polls of the late 1990s show that the qualities of character in leadership are secondary to the selfish interests of the people. Sordid lives of actors and athletes are overlooked if they entertain us and the questionable character of politicians is forgiven if they promise us what we want. After a generation of self-righteous judgment upon our leaders, our moral bankruptcy may usher in a new era of blatant self-interest in which fundamental character flaws only serve to tickle the fancy or a gain-saying public. If this is the case and history repeats itself, the same corrupting influence will eventually invade the ranks of Christian leadership and clergy. One cannot forget the times in church history when Catholic popes and Protestant preachers made a laughing stock out of a blameless character.

In this shifting climate, Kevin Mannoia strikes a prophetic note when he makes *The Integrity Factor* central to Christian leadership. Moreover, for those of us who want integrity as a "quick fix" in our redemption, he invites us on a long and torturous journey with Moses in preparation for leadership. While we remember the drama of the burning bush when Moses, the anointed, received his call to leadership, we may forget that the journey to that high moment began 40 years earlier when Moses, the fugitive, stood in doubt and despair before a desert well as his only symbol of hope.

Brought forward into contemporary experience, Mannoia takes us step by step through the journey from integrity to integrity. Drawing upon his own experience as a pastor and superintendent of pastors, as well as his studies as a scholar in the field, Mannoia begins with the integrity bestowed by Christ through conversion. This is just the beginning. Our integrity takes on maturity as life is experienced, positions are taken and decisions are made. The journey is neither short nor easy, but when we are ready, God sets a bush aflame. Then, and only then, do we see how God has been preparing us to serve Him as a leader. In that high moment, we also learn the reason for our existence. To be chosen by God as a leader of integrity is our highest trust.

We are indebted to Kevin Mannoia for taking us on this journey. Because he is still enroute himself, his writing is not hortatory, but participatory. Each of us is invited to be a fellow traveler on the road to integrity with a burning bush as our destination.

David L. McKenna

PROLOGUE

THE WELL

He looked both ways to be sure no one had seen the awful act he'd just committed. In the distance he could still see the fleeing countryman, whom he'd rescued. At his feet lay the Egyptian, pale and still with death. A purplish welt appeared on the side of the dead man's head where the rod had struck.

Moses pulled his foot from under the unmoving corpse, frantic with fear about what he'd just done. His thoughts and emotions were an out of control whirlwind welling up inside him. Before he knew it, his feet were carrying him at a dead run to the outskirts of town. The fear so controlled him that all he could think of was running – as far as he could where no one would ever find him.

As he left the edges of the city, he was finally able to force himself to think. The thought of his act once again sent his mind reeling, not with panic now but with disbelief. He slowed to a walk as questions filled his mind. How could he have done such a thing?

All he wanted to do was make the Israelites like and accept him.

Now no one would even trust him. His own foster mother would reject him for having killed one of her people. Certainly he could never appear in Pharaoh's house again. He'd been raised and was accepted there. What a privilege to have been brought up as though he were the son of Pharaoh's daughter, and now he had thrown it all away.

His own people would turn on him. Although they were slaves, the Israelites had high moral standards and murder was not looked upon kindly. He had everything going for him and now it was all wasted.

Still wandering, tears began to flood his eyes as the reality of his situation came crashing over him. Blindly he trudged on, his feet heavy with dejection and his shoulders slumped with guilt. His neck bent, face down, he was barely able to bear the immense burden.

He hardly noticed the well. It came as if from nowhere. He stumbled down the last few yards of the slope into the hollow depression to the well. Exhausted from the inner turmoil of the past few hours, his body ached to rest. He collapsed on the broken-down stone edge of the well, his body and spirit racked under the pressure of his circumstances.

Sitting amidst the rubble of the well's edge, his mind swirled with the events of the recent past. As the images of that moment on the street played over in his mind, he could not shake the vision of the dead body at his feet, its sightless eyes searing his mind, and the edges of the Israelite's robe flapping in the wind as he ran from the scene.

Total abandonment. That's what he felt. Nowhere to go. No home. No one who would claim him. He would be ostracized and rejected by the only people he knew. Not only had his deed severed his relationship with those who had raised him, but it had dashed forever any hope of being accepted by his own people.

He was alone. That was the painful part. How could someone be so highly regarded in the courts of Pharaoh one moment and be so alone the next? He had actually been enjoying the new acceptance which his Israelite countrymen had begun to give him. Now to have it ripped from his grasp and destroyed by one thoughtless deed was like a knife penetrating his heart.

How long he was at the well he did not know. Hours? Probably days. It all ran together. He didn't keep track. That wasn't important. The well was the only place he knew now. The bottom of this depression had become familiar to him. But as time wore on, he gradually came to an awareness of reality and his need to move on. He didn't know what he should do, he just knew he had to do something – go somewhere. He couldn't stay any longer. Staying meant death. He wasn't sure why or even where the feeling came from, but he sensed within himself a battle. One part of him wanted to give up and die at this broken-down well in this depression. On the other hand he felt the urge to go. But where?

With a final sense of release, Moses let the desire to remain at the well loosen its death grip in favor of the increasingly strong sense of call to move on. He struggled to his feet with a tiny spark of energy from some mysterious and unknown source.

Slowly he moved away. Making his way up the slope of the depression was not easy. It required every ounce of energy. It seemed as though the emotional and physical battle had drained him of all energy in his will. Somehow he managed to reach the rim. He paused and glanced back at the well. It had been his place – his only place. In a way, he hated to leave, yet he knew he must. He never wanted to see that well again. It was too painful, too comfortable, too alluring, too broken down. He had to press on. He turned and faced the horizon ahead. Where would he go and what would he do? He didn't know, only that he had to go – out there, anywhere, to something, somewhere; just out there – on a journey.

INTRODUCTION

The day Moses came to the well was a bad day for him. Before that, he had learned the system of politics and control in Egypt and had developed networks and relationships. He had watched up close as Pharaoh lead the nation, and learned to do the things that leaders do. Moses had even begun to assert himself as the deliverer of his people. But on that day he hit a wall. His identity crushed, he was without recourse as to his future. The ability and talent he thought he possessed had failed miserably and proved inadequate.

Moses' journey of rewiring his identity began at the well. It was the beginning of rediscovering the foundation on which any activity of leadership should be built. Could that rewiring have happened in Egypt? Perhaps, but we will never know. Only God knows whether what He did in Moses could have been accomplished another way.

The well marked the beginning of Moses' 40 years wandering in the wilderness. Of course we do not know exactly what went on in those years. I think it is rather safe to say, however, that the wilderness experience was life changing. It peeled away Moses' confidence in the skills he had learned in Egypt that had become the basis of his self-worth and identity. Moses was forced to come face-to-face with who he was. Layer upon layer of self-justification were peeled away through isolation, loneliness, times of introspection and quietness.

At some point in that wilderness Moses came to accept the reality that, although he had been prepared and destined in the very courts of Pharaoh for leadership, what he now experienced in aimless wandering and shepherding may be his ultimate destiny. Can you imagine the questions that consumed him? "God, is this all there is? I thought I was to be a deliverer. Why did I receive the upbringing I've had, only to wander in the wilderness? What are your plans for me, God?"

Whether it took 40 years for that process to occur we don't know. What we do know is that Moses finally came to stand before the bush and was confronted with the reality of his being. He was incapable of leadership merely through self-assertion in activities and was stripped of position. Obviously his confidence in his own ability to exercise the kind of leadership he had seen and had been trained to perform was badly shaken.

At the bush, for the first time, Moses was confronted with the choice of whom he would serve. Doubtless it was a struggle of the wills. Even his own resistance to God's call was simply a rationalization of why he was incapable of performing the duties that God expected of him. God, however, pressing the point, made it clear that the choice before Moses had nothing to do with his abilities or learned skills. It had to do with the foundation on which his identity would be built and out of which his leadership activity would flow. He was being called to serve God.

With the bush behind him, God began to put back the layers of activities in Moses' life. These activities are what people would see in Moses' daily living. It is by looking at these activities that others would consider him to be a great man. God gave him back the ability to communicate, to confront, to make decisions, to manage and to lead. All these abilities were the basis on which those who watched him deemed him to be a great leader, yet all these things were now wrapped around a core identity shaped as a servant of God.

During the wilderness experience, between the well and the bush, God peeled away Moses' dependence on his outward activities as the basis for his leadership. He took away Moses' core identity which was based on his own skills and abilities and replaced it with an identity rooted in being a servant of God. Up to this point, Moses had based his life on talents and abilities he had learned in Pharaoh's court. Now he was called to base his life on who he was before God. The talents and abilities he had would then be far more effective. That is the process of leadership formation which becomes foundational to the Christian leader.

Chapter

1

THE
PARADIGM
OF FORMATION

LEADERSHIP DEFINED

As the church enters a new era, the focus of attention is shifting to the role and importance of leadership. Books are being written and seminars taught on the subject. Churches are looking for it and organizations demand it. What that ideal blend of skills and gifts actually looks like is different with each book and seminar, yet somehow we know it when we see it. And usually it's closely related to performance. In other words, where you find good results, there you'll find a leader out front.

Although those in leadership positions must be particularly sensitive to this new emphasis on leadership, every Christian must accept the label of leader to the extent that he or she becomes salt and light to the world. Jesus has called each member of His body to positively influence others around them. Through their influence Christians are called to lead others to faith and life in Christ.

Simply put then, leadership means influencing others. Every Christian and every Christian organization is called to a leadership role in some sphere. Whether individually or corporately, the Christian objective is to impact the world for Christ. For you individually, that may mean your neighbor, your coworker, your family member or your friend. For the Christian organization, it may mean a region, a city or a community. Whatever sphere, it means projecting an influence to cause change – change for Christ and His kingdom. Leadership for Christians and Christian organizations does not mean that they merely accept the terrible, deteriorating conditions of society while wringing their spiritual hands in a "holier than thou" attitude. It involves a positive influence to cause change.

Consider the difference between a thermometer and a thermostat. Doubtless you've had experience with both and know their use. The thermometer has the task of measuring the environmental conditions of a room so we know how hot or cold it is. It tells us the temperature outside so we can respond appropriately with a heavy coat or short sleeves. It reacts to the air around it and simply tells us what it's like.

The thermostat, on the other hand, not only exists to be affected by its environment but has available to it the enormous power to change the environment as necessary. You determine that you want a 72 degree environment. When the room cools to 68 degrees, the thermostat says, "This isn't what was intended." It starts the furnace and changes the room temperature. It not only diagnoses the environment but also changes it. You tell me – which one represents the leader?

The future of any organization rises or falls on leadership. The role of those asked to give leadership has risen to unprecedented importance. The quality and effectiveness of the organization is directly attributable to those who lead it. I've often said that within 3-5 years an organization will take on the characteristics of its leader and begin to "look" like him or her. It's a sobering thought. That is why a lot of attention is currently being given to developing leaders. Most of it is designed to "equip" leaders for their task. As a result, a flood of resources is available in areas like time management, leadership theory, management, administration, conflict resolution and strategic planning to name a few. These are extremely important and leaders should certainly acquire and improve these skills in performing their duty.

My priority, however, is not to focus on "equipping" spiritual leaders with visible tools for their position but, rather, on the unseen building blocks of "empowerment." I want to prick the minds of those engaged in leadership activities and call them to give attention to the foundation from which their activities will proceed. That's not to say that task-oriented equipping is not good. It's just to say that no amount of skill acquisition for tasks or activities will ever replace the need for healthy and proper foundations which give those skills meaning and effectiveness. My father calls it "tending the well" out of which our performance of activities will flow. If a well is not regularly "tended," soon the sides will crumble, the water will become impure, and eventually it will fill in and be good for nothing. My desire is to help you "tend" the foundations out of which your leadership tasks will flow so they will be fresh, pure and effective.

TWO DIMENSIONS OF LEADERSHIP

Let me make the point this way. There are two levels which comprise leadership. The upper level deals with equipping leaders for visible activity and performance. The lower level deals with empowerment for unseen identity. It's like an iceberg on the ocean. When you look at an iceberg, you're only seeing one-tenth of its mass. Nine-tenths of the iceberg is actually beneath the water level, out of public view. It's hidden, unseen.

This unseen part gives the whole iceberg its stability and features. When winter storms blow and the seas are high, this unseen part of the iceberg keeps it from capsizing or even breaking up. Without it, the iceberg would be tossed about by every wind and wave. People traveling by on ships and planes cannot see the mass beneath the water. But it's there, providing a stable foundation for the one-tenth that protrudes into the visible area.

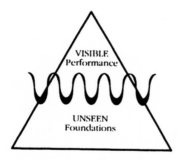

Let's examine the iceberg analogy a bit further. Notice that in a normal iceberg, the center of gravity is somewhere beneath the waterline. That's why it can withstand the storms above the water. But what would happen if we changed the shape of the iceberg? Imagine it as a square. The center of gravity would move upward toward the visible area above the water. It would become much more susceptible to the storms. If we actually inverted the iceberg, the gravity center would be above water level making it highly unstable and precariously balanced on a small foundation.

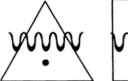 

Leadership formation recognizes this dynamic interrelationship between identity (bottom of the iceberg) and activity (top of the iceberg). As long as leaders intentionally "tend the well" of their identity through the paths of formation, their "center of gravity" will remain solidly below the water line. That's the source of their confidence and stability when circumstances in the organization around them are pressing, pushing or demanding. As a leader, then, you are able to meet performance expectations with a proper perspective. In other words, when you are successful in your performance, a well-formed identity reminds you that visible success for success' sake is not necessarily success in kingdom terms. Defining success as simply having the largest salary, the biggest church, the hottest yearly reports is not the product of well-formed leadership foundations. Yet we naturally tend to evaluate success in these terms. Keeping the iceberg in balance keeps this kind of natural human tendency in check.

I recall a particular case of a talented Christian leader who saw amazing results in his ministry. Everything he touched turned to gold. His organization skyrocketed. All his statistics were up, people praised him, and they extolled him on the radio for the great performance. Other leaders traveled to see what was happening firsthand. They hoped they could find a clue to take home with them. They'd be happy with just a fraction of his success. This leader was good. Everybody knew it – and so did he. An attitude of intolerant arrogance began to creep in under the superficial spiritual activities. What devastation when immoral behavior suddenly became known. Why? He had everything going for him. How could he have been so successful yet so false?

We've all seen it. Perhaps it happened close to home or on television. Wherever it happens, the pattern is the same. Success in activities and performance begins to define leaders' identity to such a degree that they cease tending the well of the unseen identity. Their center of gravity begins to move up as their foundation in the unseen realm shrinks. Either they think it can't happen to them because they're too valuable to the kingdom, or they think they are above such temptations. Building their identity on their successful performance places them on a fast track to burnout, moral failure or a false sense of security.

Conversely, leaders sometimes fail to meet performance expectations in "doing their task." In fact, failure to perform may be more common than success. The bottom line doesn't look good. Year end reports are "southbound." The expectations of our overseer, our board or ourselves are not being met. If the center of gravity in the leader is found in a well-formed foundation beneath the waterline, his or her identity need not be broken. Yet, it may be a painful and difficult situation to accept. We are human and experience pain and disappointment. But leaders can weather such circumstances and even undergo career adjustments without being threatened in the core of who they are.

It doesn't take long in reading leadership material to find a case of unmet expectations. One that I had to deal with occurred a few years back, early in my ministry as an overseer. The pastor was likable, humorous, sincere and knew all the church-growth principles there were to know. His friends were all successful and he wanted nothing more than to see his church grow. He went to seminars, read books, applied the principles, but it never seemed to produce the results he wanted. At gatherings of pastors he would weep for growth. All his emotions strained to implore God's blessing through increases, yet it never came.

No one suspected anything until a concerned friend called and said, "Kevin, our pastor is moving out and leaving his wife and family." Why? He looked so sincere. He said the right words. He had all the principles. Yet in doing all the right activities, his performance expectations had not been met. He had built his very identity on his ability to perform. When success didn't happen, his identity was broken, his behavior changed, and he sought emotional affirmation with another woman. He couldn't meet the performance expectations on which his identity was built, so his identity collapsed.

Perhaps the troubling times have nothing to do with unmet expectations. Maybe there are simply difficulties or disagreements with people in the group. People begin to get agitated and start taking pot shots, attacking and accusing in an effort to register their disapproval. What do you think will be their target? The leader, of course – *you!* The criticism will usually focus on procedures or methods. That's only natural. Since your activities and methods are visible, people will notice them, evaluate them and disagree with them. If a ship full of armed hunters were sailing by an iceberg and they decided to start some target practice, which part of the berg would they shoot? The top, of course.

Yet when criticism comes from people, unfortunately their intent is often to do damage to your identity, your heart, your core. If you have a deeply rooted, properly formed identity, you will come through the storm largely unscathed, perhaps a bit wounded, with a few "holes" shot in the "top of the iceberg" but stabilized and whole nonetheless.

Imagine, however, that you have neglected the weighty issues of identity. What happens when you remove the bottom of the iceberg? It capsizes, doesn't it? What used to be above the waterline now becomes what keeps it afloat. Identity is based on performance and activity. When things are not going well and the external expectations are not met, identity begins to crumble. In this case, who we are has been based on what we do and how well we do it. When challenged or when faced with career adjustments, defensiveness sets in as a natural reaction to protect who we are.

In this case, not only is our performance being questioned but so is our identity. The leader usually assumes that the governing board is being unjust and is basing its actions on personal dislike. Such a feeling is very real to the leader since for all practical purposes he or she has allowed his or her identity to become synonymous with activity. No matter how hard the overseer or board may try, they may never succeed in convincing the leader that a career adjustment is not an attack on his or her personal identity.

It is ultimately our own responsibility to pursue a balance between identity and activity. Our overseer can facilitate it, but he or she cannot do it for us. I am responsible for the balance in my life, to pursue a well-formed paradigm of leadership, and to "tend the well" of my identity as foundational to all I do in the visible arena of performing my task. What people in our organizations see is the top of the iceberg. They see the leader simply doing the visible activities of leadership. Those activities, for the most part, are the tasks or behaviors which can be measured and evaluated. How well does he manage time? Does she affirm enough? Does he delegate cleanly? Is she producing enough widgets?

Because these kinds of things are so obvious, we equate successful leadership with doing them well and in large quantities. Hence, we evaluate leaders by these criteria. The problem is that such a limited perspective further affirms our false assumption that effective leaders perform activities successfully. That's only the top of the iceberg.

Remember Moses? His first efforts at leadership failed because he assumed he merely had to do what he had learned as a leader in training. Have you ever known leaders who washed out, burned out or checked out because they couldn't take the stress of performance expectations? Somehow, they bought into the idea that only performance counts – the top of the iceberg. Somebody set the standard for them, and they were convinced that if they didn't measure up, then they weren't good.

Who they are becomes synonymous with what they do and how well they do it. They have been caught in a performance-based attitude that equates leadership only with tasks. They've forgotten the deeper, unseen side of leadership which is its foundation. They forgot to "tend the well" from which their performance flows. This is the bottom of the iceberg, their foundation and identity. No amount of skill training through seminars, books or classes will make up for this deficit.

Generally we could say that equipping and empowering represent the top and bottom of the iceberg. To use another analogy, they are two indispensable sides of the same coin. Leaders should not emphasize the development of one over the other. The tendency of our contemporary, performance-based culture, however, is to categorize and define leadership as an objectifiable profession, even in its Christian context. Good leaders, then, are defined as people who can show a good bottom line, or quarterly report or a growth chart that's "northbound." It's easy to fall into the trap of equating these qualities with good leadership. The result is that soon our very definition of leadership shrinks. This tendency causes us to focus on the visible activity of leadership to such a degree that the foundational elements are lost in the rush to succeed. We've spent so much time learning top-of-the-iceberg activities that we've forgotten the bottom-of-the-iceberg foundations.

LEADERSHIP FORMATION

You've probably heard and read a great deal these days about "spiritual formation." Similarly you've doubtless been exposed to material dealing with "leadership development." Usually they are addressed as separate pursuits. Each is a discipline all its own. The former usually deals with personal spiritual maturity, while the latter deals with position or personal influence.

Generally, you would think that spiritual formation addresses the bottom of the iceberg while leadership development would concentrate on the top. While there is truth to that assumption, it remains too compartmentalized. I want to introduce you to "Leadership Formation" which is the careful but intentional integration of these two pursuits, uniquely patterned in Scripture for every Christian leader.

Giving ourselves to the foundations of leadership formation becomes all the more urgent when you consider the overwhelming pain and brokenness sweeping through the lives of leaders. Broken homes and marriages, dysfunctional relationships and families, and warped perceptions of ministry and leadership all emit from a misplaced yearning for success in performance. The response to this trauma and pain should not be the devisement of more complex seminars or courses focused on the symptom. Rather, it should be to thoroughly search the foundations of identity from which such behavior proceeds. These painful symptoms usually require attention to the unseen foundation. I once heard an experienced pastor say that whenever someone came to him with problems, he treated them as symptoms and probed deeper to the next level until he found the source of the trouble.

Problems that surface in the observable struc-
ture of a building are often the result of a faulty but
unseen foundation. Likewise, the visible performance
of Christian leaders will be strained and eventually crack
unless awareness and care are given to the unseen foundation. In the Southern California area, it's not uncommon to hear of homes or businesses which become
unusable when the foundation is damaged in an earth-
quake. No amount of paint or plaster will make up for
a damaged foundation. So we cannot simply increase
the frequency and intensity of our focus on methodol-
ogy. Attempting to alter behavior is merely addressing
the tip of the iceberg while ignoring the unseen mass
beneath the surface which gives the "tip" its character
and stability.

Talking about leadership in this way cuts across
the grain of our human nature. We tend to observe
behavior and then imitate. We look around for the leadership patterns that are most visibly successful and replicate them in our own context. What we see, however,
is the pattern of behavior in the top of the iceberg –
performance.

Because success in the secular world is more
easily measurable than in the church, it often becomes
the model we use. It's easy to tell if a secular business

is successful. Is it going out of business? Growing? Making money? Expanding franchises? We assume the ones that are successful must be doing something we should be doing to expand the church or Christian organizations. Hence we replicate the leadership patterns and behavior of secular organizations in the Christian context. We ask, "What would the corporate CEO do to handle this situation?" Don't misunderstand me. I'm not saying this is entirely a wrong approach. Certainly there is room to learn from the success of the business world, but there is a limit. IBM, Chrysler and Microsoft cannot become the standard by which we pattern our activities and judge our performance.

To superimpose secular leadership patterns on the church leads to a process of sanctifying the secular. True, it has happened in many other arenas; however, in this regard "a horse by any other name is still a horse." Secular leadership styles and activities cannot be separated from their inherently secular foundations. Certainly at a superficial level no apparent problem exists.

However, as circumstances arise which test the leadership and force it to rely on its character and nature, conflict begins to surface. Although in the visible performance area there will be much we can learn from secular business, remember that under every visible tip there is an unseen foundation which guides that performance. We may find ourselves making pragmatic decisions based on leadership policies which we have replicated from secular patterns, but which compromise the fundamental character of the church.

We must be cautious and insightful in attempting to unequally yoke leadership patterns which are tried and true in the secular organization with the Christian organism. The organismic nature of the church gives it a unique nature that requires a unique paradigm of leadership.

The secular leadership paradigm emphasizes function, results and performance. It says to would-be leaders, "learn the system" in an attempt to replicate results. Spiritual leadership must emphasize character, essence and nature while saying, "become." At this point, spiritual leadership asserts itself as counter-culture and stands in stark contrast, and often opposition, to the basic elements of secular leadership. Becoming this kind of leader, then, is a process. Rooted in Scripture and largely dealing with the unseen dimension of identity, it is a journey in leadership formation.

Chapter

2

THE
DOWNWARD
PATH

BEGINNING THE JOURNEY

I remember well the carefully-laid plans for my future. At age 19, everything seemed bright and possible. I would go to the right school, work for a powerful congressman and move into the State Department so that one day I would be an ambassador. Arrangements had been made, relationships established and timelines determined. My upbringing, personality, experiences and contacts all seemed to provide impeccable qualifications. Then came the tap on the shoulder through the quiet but clear impulse of the Holy Spirit. Would I serve God wholly? Could I really see myself outside the circle of complete, full-time ministry? Would I even be willing to do what I had thought I would not, like be a pastor or missionary? Understand, I had the highest respect for these, as my parents were both.

I decided I'd do it. No fireworks, bands or celebrations. The manifestation of that decision was simply a quick visit to the registrar's office at Roberts Wesleyan College in order to change my major. That ignoble act, however, set me on an inexorable journey

downward. By "downward" I do not mean humiliating
or embarrassingly unsuccessful. I simply mean a process of leadership formation after the pattern of Jesus.

What many Christians cling to in following Christ
is His behavior of loving gentility, single-minded boldness or holy righteousness. They observe His behavior,
and in an effort to be a good follower, strive to imitate
Him. How many times have you heard someone ask,
"What would Jesus do?" as a way to deal with the problems they're living with. They think that if they replicate His behavior in a similar circumstance, all will be
well. What they're missing is the fact that there is a
deeper side to Jesus out of which those behaviors flow.
The Christian leader begins to discover that deeper side
on the downward path. Answering the call to leadership may mean becoming a pastor, a teacher, a busi-
nessman or even an ambassador. In any case, it
effectively begins the process of forming that deeper
character which eventually will allow for a natural flow
of behaviors after the pattern of Jesus. If our character
and identity have been formed after the pattern of Christ,
then the behavior which flows from it will also be
Christlike. As I heard a friend once say, "We always
behave out of our identity."

However, this deeper side is not always so appealing. Sometimes the process of shaping our charac-

ter is painful. It certainly was for Jesus. It might be
considered the dark side, the unattractive side, the distasteful side. Yet, upon closer scrutiny, we can see that
it is as much a part of the character of Jesus as wetness
is the character of water. This downward path is, at first
glance, unpalatable if not repulsive to the human will.
Yet, it is required in order for solid leadership foundations to be built out of which performance will flow.

There is a deep joy somewhere inside, but the
circumstances out of which God shapes our identity
may not be the happiest. Joy, you see, proceeds from
the inner confidence and peace of God at work in us.
Happiness, on the other hand, comes from external
circumstances which may change over time. Leadership formation may not be appealing, because while
there is joy at being a servant of God, the process may
not be entirely happy. But do not be dissuaded. Start-
ing on the journey of leadership formation allows us
the joy of putting on the pattern of Christ.

If our master teacher is Jesus, then we must
begin where He began, which was – the incarnation,
of course. Not the physical incarnation of the Gospels,
but what I consider the real, unseen incarnation in
Philippians chapter 2. Christ started at this point, and
so must we. We cannot deal with leadership without
dealing with incarnation. It's an inextricable part of lead-

ership formation. In His incarnational "downward path," Jesus forever set the pattern for Christian leadership in opposition to the world.

HAVE THIS MIND IN YOU

"**H**ave this mind in you," says Paul, "which was in Jesus Christ ..." He's not saying we should simply do activities that might appear Christlike. Wondering what action Christ would take in a particular circumstance and then doing it is simply to mimic activity. The natural consequence is that eventually our perception of what Christ might do becomes blurred and intermixed with our own preferences. We may project our desires onto Christ's behavior in order to justify our own behavior. We wind up doing what we want to do under the pretense that Christ Himself would do it that way. That's called rationalizing. We might do things in the name of Christlikeness when He would rather have nothing to do with such activity.

Imitating activity is not the answer. A total transformation of the mind is required such that actions become merely the telltale signs of the inner nature. Identity naturally flows into activity. Behavior flows from nature. Putting on the mind of Christ, therefore, does not mean exerting our will by doing more or better activities. What it means is a simple but complete surrender of our will. Although surrender is inconsistent with human nature, it is prerequisite to putting on this new mind. Our tendency is self-improvement by setting our jaw, pulling up our bootstraps and resolving to work harder, do more or act better. We go to another seminar, buy the latest book or take another class. Assuming that real success as leaders begins with doing things better, we pursue improvement.

What we need is not improvement of our behavior but replacement of our nature. We are not called to imitate actions. We are called to a transformed mind (Romans 12:2), to put on a new nature like our Master's (Colossians 3:10), and to put on the mind of Christ (Philippians 2:5). Transformed identity always leads to transformed activity. Paul says, "Put off the old nature with its practices and put on the new nature." He does not tell us to put off practices as a means to changing our nature. A changed nature leads to changed behavior, not the other way around.

This radical transformation of nature is painful and, in fact, impossible for the human will to accomplish. Our only recourse is to surrender. Not to be confused with apathetic lethargy, this surrender is an intense commitment of the will to undergo serious metamorphosis in order to be remolded in the image of Christ. It begins on the same downward path that Christ Himself took.

EMPTIED FOR SERVICE

Jesus Christ held every claim to all the characteristics of God. He was after all, one with the Father. Without Him nothing was made that was made. He was equal with God. He had incredible rights as God, yet He did not cling tenaciously to that position as something which needed to be defended. He was willing to let go of everything to which He was entitled, including His identity. As He did, He began His downward journey.

"Release" is the key word to the downward path. Release of personal position, rights, possessions, and most importantly, identity. Someone else's agenda becomes more important than our own, and we choose to release our own plans. Through this total release, Christ emptied Himself for service to God (Philippians 2:7). To serve God would have been impossible had there been any remnant of His own will or position which required defending. The true servant is devoid of any personal identity or ambition which would conflict with that of their master. They are truly emptied.

It is not easy to be emptied for the service of someone else. The human will clings desperately to everything it can amass for self-justification and exaltation. We build priorities around our will, and accomplish personal ambitions by our will. Our identity is rooted in our will which is the center of our being and gives energy to life. For the very core of our being to undergo a change of nature is, at best, excruciatingly painful.

It's like the core of an onion that has built up layer upon layer of defenses to protect and justify itself. Those layers of self-justification take the form of ambitions, plans, goals, attitudes and habits. There's really nothing wrong with those things except when they exist to prop up or stroke our self-centered will. Peeling away the layers of behavior which have built up in an effort to justify and defend the "self-will" is in direct conflict with its defensive nature. That's why it is impossible to do.

When we come to the point of making the willful commitment to be transformed – to put on a new nature, to have the mind of Christ – the most we can hope for is a "huge sigh," and a literal release to God's Spirit. It may sound trite and perhaps super spiritual, but there is a clear spiritual, emotional and sometimes physical "letting go" that has to happen. Try enjoying the thrill of parachuting sometime without letting go of the handle on the jump plane. It simply can't be done. God guarantees that once you choose to release, a spark of energy from some apparently mysterious source will propel you forward to the unknown horizon where ultimately you will find confidence in that new identity.

Don't be surprised at this point, though, if you find yourself trying to retake control. You can't expect that in one moment or event you have learned all there is to know about the downward path to the mind of Christ. None of us has. Crisis points occur when our initial choice to release is tested. Circumstances will come regularly which will tempt us to reassert control over our own destiny – to take back control, to once again serve our own agenda. Remember how often Jesus got away to pray? How strong the temptation must have been to call angels to deliver Him or establish Him as king! Yet, in those times alone in communion with the Father, I expect He was reaffirming His commitment of release, surrender and identity as a servant of God.

In my case, I immediately set about laying new plans and agendas on this new course God had given me. "So, God, you want me to give up my well-laid plans in order to serve you wholly? Fine. No problem. I'll do it." Release. My next move? "Where's the top of the heap in ministry, and how do I get there?" I proceeded to lay out educational, family and professional goals in five year increments through age 40 (back then that seemed a long way off).

My initial surrender, manifested by a change of major in the registrar's office, was only the first step. It was the top layer; the journey had only begun. Regular releases had to follow. At each step I would accept the new direction and quickly lay my own new plans on that course. Time after time God said, "This!" and I said, "OK, that. But I'll do it my way." In this manner, event after event, year after year, God peels away the layers of ambition and self-justification in order to get at the core and rewire us from the inside out. Think back in your own journey and you may find the same process.

You say, "There'll be nothing left of me!" In reality, God puts back in place new layers of activity, performance, ambition and agendas to replace the old.

In many cases they may be exactly the same – just wrapped around a new identity, core and motivation. Many of your goals may be realized, but now they proceed from a different motivation. Recognize, however, that you and I will regularly be confronted with circumstances where we are tempted to take back control. The choice to release and surrender will be tested often in leadership and must be reaffirmed.

Ah, but I'm jumping ahead. We're still on the downward path which moves us toward a new identity through putting on the mind of Christ. What's the objective of this emptying process? Certainly it helps to understand the result. Jesus emptied Himself to become a servant. But a servant of whom?

We may mistakenly think He came to be our servant. We, then, who are being formed in like-mindedness, also pursue the role of servant to people. But committing ourselves to serve people misses the essential nature of the mind we are called to adopt. In reality, Christ did not come to serve people but to serve the Father. He came to minister to people as a manifestation of His service to His Father.

I know, you are immediately thinking of Matthew 20:28, "The Son of Man came not to be served but to serve." Actually it says that the Son of Man came not to be "ministered unto" but to "minister." There's a big difference between ministering to someone and being their servant. Most notably, being someone's servant means you release your agenda in favor of theirs as a source of personal identity. Can you imagine trying to be this kind of servant to the people you lead? You'd be like a dog chasing its tail in a pointless and vain attempt to please all of your people. You would tear yourself apart and your identity would be shattered since it's an impossible task.

As with Jesus, leaders are called to serve one master, not many. His motivation was to serve God which, of necessity, compelled Him to minister with His life to those around Him, thereby influencing their lives. In committing Himself to serve His father, Jesus allowed the Father's agenda to become His own. What was important to the Father was important to Him. The passion of the Father's heart propelled Him to act and guided His behavior. What was the Father's agenda? To minister to the needs of people, especially reconciling them back to Himself.

With the commitment to serve another comes the reality that their agenda becomes more important than our own. If we serve people, their agendas will supplant ours and ultimately our primary goal will be to please them. Following that process to its logical extension means that we become what others want us to become. That opens the door to internal conflict, burnout and depression when we are unable to please people with conflicting agendas. Confidence, self-esteem and spiritual power give way to manipulative techniques. In that case our goal is to please people, making them happy and keeping peace in the group at all costs. This scenario assumes that effectiveness as a leader means merely meeting the desires of everyone. But listen! That's management, not leadership. That's becoming a slave to others, not a servant of God.

If we serve God, His transcendent agenda will become the guide for our activities. That may create friction when we encounter conflicting human agendas. Quiet and unperturbed confidence prevails, however, when we know we are faithfully serving our Master and fulfilling His agenda of ministering to people. We do what we see our Master doing. What's important to Him is important to us. His compulsion to love and minister to people prevents our ministry activity from taking on a callous attitude of superiority. Thus, on the downward path we are to empty ourselves in order that we may become servants of God, driven and guided in ministry not by our will, but by His.

Being a servant of God has little to do with activity and much to do with identity. Who we are is based neither on what we do nor how many we please, but on Whom we serve. For the servant of God, identity is rooted in God, not self, performance, station or popularity. The resulting confidence is reconciled to humility in spirit, inasmuch as the sovereign, just and holy power of the God whom we serve is, at the same time, gentle, meek and loving. We neither become a doormat for others to walk on at will, nor do we become high-handed and abusive of other people in doing our work. Humble gentility and loving meekness characterize our identity, since that's the nature of God. The confidence which comes from that identity translates into bold, single-minded activity as we are driven in leadership by the One whom we serve.

HUMBLED IN OBEDIENCE

 further step on the downward path to l e a d e r s h i p patterned after Christ takes the form of humbling ourselves in obedience. While emptying deals with our identity, humbling deals with our will. We empty ourselves of our own identity through

the release of our rights. We humble ourselves by bowing our will.

Because humbling ourselves requires a bowing or breaking of the will, it is something which requires a willful decision of obedience to God. In it we submit our will to the Father's will for us. Anything less than a full, uncompromising submission to God preempts the possibility of His will being accomplished in and through us. The Scriptures are replete with warnings that we cannot engage in the pursuit of our will and God's at the same time. Our lives will be given to one or the other. Ours is only to decide whom we will serve. God is not pushy. His desire is that we serve Him wholly, that we "sell out" to Him. That was His intention from the start, but He's left the choice to us. He will respect our right to assert our own will as we please. He will not usurp control. He will take it only if we willfully and humbly give it.

This is not a "once-made, always-made" decision. It, like any other passion of the flesh, must be disciplined through the regular practice of bowing our will to that of God's. We cannot assume that we will be able to perform such an act of submission without practice. When a crisis point comes, don't think that you can submit to God without having made a regular habit of surrender to Him.

If you believe you can live daily with an attitude of personal control, pursuing your ambitions and still be able to submit to God on the big issues, you're gravely mistaken. You overestimate the intentions of our human will and underestimate the impact of our fallen nature. It is only through regular and consistent decisions of release and submission of our will to God's that a pattern is established which epitomizes a transformed mind and allows the will of God to be fully activated in and through us. In other words, doing your "own thing" during the easy times and thinking you can let go to God in the crisis is a fatal mistake. That's like saying, "I won't develop my legs during training times, but on race day I'll run the marathon."

When I was young and had a crew cut, my cowlick presented no problem. When I let my hair get longer, however, it took regular attention, tubes of hair creme, bobby pins and even a nylon stocking each night to get that stubborn hair to "bow" to my will. Finally it was tamed. Yet, even today it occasionally requires some "breaking." Notice in your daily life and leadership the regular temptation and tendency to reassert personal control. Notice, also, how those times usually come when we have neglected the bottom of the iceberg – our identity as a servant of God, emptied and humbled to Him.

The downward path to leadership does not appear to make sense within the context of an activity-based culture where terms such as higher, bigger, control, more, better and upward characterize success. As a matter of fact, for us to suggest that the path to true leadership takes us downward to surrender, release, obedience and emptying is incompatible, if not counter, to our culture. Yet the kingdom which God through Christ came to establish is precisely that – counter-culture. It goes against the grain of our human nature – defend yourself and pursue your ambitions. It collides with societal expectations – assert yourself and grab power. It counters secular patterns of leadership – make yourself successful by increasing your control. It undermines worldly educational assumptions – develop yourself as the highest priority.

At the root of leadership formation is the call to have the same mind which was also in Christ. It is characterized by the downward path. He submitted to the Father to become a servant; we must submit to God to become a servant. He submitted to the Father to establish His kingdom; we must submit to God to establish *His* kingdom. He submitted to the point of death; we must submit to the point of death.

In the ancient covenant-making process, the covenant partners engaged in the "walk of death" around the sacrificed animal. A pure, unblemished animal was selected to be sacrificed. This sacrifice would seal the covenant being made. The animal was killed and cut in half lengthwise. From this process came the Hebrew phrase "to cut a covenant." The covenant partners would stand at either end of the sacrificial offering. Each person walked around and between the parts of the animal in a figure 8 pattern. This was the walk of death. It symbolized denial of self for the sake of the covenant partner.

The firepot of Genesis 15 represented God forming covenant with Abraham. Abraham did not walk the walk of death on that day, however. His walk occurred when God called, "Go to a new land." Abraham said, "But God, where to? Why?" And God said, "Go, Abraham." "But God, my family is happy and settled." "Go, Abraham." "But God, my land, business, relationships, connections are all here." God again said, "Go Abraham." Still the desire to control remained. "But God, you don't understand. My possessions, ambition, agenda and plans are here." And still God said, "Release them all, Abraham, and go!" Finally Abraham obeyed. Abraham's walk of death occurred when he released his land, plans, priorities, ambitions and personal dreams, and traveled to unknown places in obedience to God.

Throughout His life, Jesus was confronted with the choice of achieving His ends through His own will or obediently serving the Father. It required emptying and humbling. It took Him to His greatest struggle in the Garden of Gethsemane. His choice? "Father, not my will but thine be done!"

By His life and death Jesus set the pattern of Christian priorities in opposition to the world forever. Every spiritual leader must follow, for indeed "you are serving the Lord Christ" (Colossians 3:24).

Chapter

3

THE
RUGGED
PATH

FACING IDENTITY

The phone call came like a lifeline to a drowning swimmer. The president of a strong Christian college said, "I'd like for you to consider coming as vice president." Talk about tempting. How easy it would've been to say "yes." My family and I were on a five-day driving tour visiting many of the churches under my care. In a way I think I had planned the trip purposely to be away in order to "lick my wounds." I had been in the middle of foreclosing on a church in serious default, and they didn't like it; trying to keep open communication with a pastor who was angry with me; dealing with a church seriously divided in a fight; fielding accusations of selfish manipulation at my own church; trying to salvage a broken relationship with one of my staff; and still attempting to cast a vision for forward ministry. Needless to say I was "under it" and breaking fast.

It hurt, too. People we had counted as dear friends were clearly upset with me. People in whom we had invested time, energy, tears and our lives were "disengaging" from us. Leaders I'd confided in and trusted for advice were using that knowledge against me. What in the world was going on? As you understand, words on a page or paragraphs in a book like this fail to describe the full measure of times like these. All I could do was work overtime trying to figure out what I was doing to create such difficulties. Sound familiar? Have you been there before? It's like a rugged path to an unknown destination.

That's when the call came. We weren't even at home when the college president caught up with me. So there was no opportunity to be emotionally swayed by familiar surroundings. Emotionally, mentally and even physically we were removed from the things that would be natural attachments. It was as if God really wanted to test a point. He made sure the point was unequivocally clear by means of the exaggerated circumstances.

How easy to cut loose and move to the security of a strong institution, a cozy community, a new environment, a healthy salary – "out there," anywhere but "here." Yet, through it all I couldn't help but let the words of my critics push me to accept some possible truth in them, and more importantly, get to the bottom line issues: "Who am I to think that, on force of will, I can make all things right? Who am I, indeed?" That was the real question this rugged path forced into my consciousness. Was I, Kevin Mannoia, strategic leader, catalyst and fixer of the woes of an ailing district? Was I a talented implementer of my priorities and caster of my vision, albeit for the altruistic purpose of building the church? Or was there more?

In the Interfaith Chapel at the Houston Intercontinental Airport between flights, it hit me like a lightening bolt: I was Kevin Mannoia, servant of God; nothing more and nothing less. That was the "hollow of the well." There began a journey of discovering the principles of leadership formation after the pattern of Christ – Himself a servant of God.

The way of Christ is not easy. Leadership formation is not for the faint or half-hearted. Not that God is attempting to make such a life as difficult as possible. It's simply that the counter-culture nature of traveling the downward path places us at odds with the natural flow of our surroundings. Conflict is created as the world attempts to mold us according to its standards, while we are pledged to a different master. It's hardly a wonder, then, that God so often speaks encouragement to those committed to serving Him. He recognizes the conflict and understands our need when we're in the middle of it.

Knowing that with adversity comes the strong temptation to retake control of our circumstances and destiny, He urges us: "Commit your way to the Lord; trust in Him and He will act" (Psalms 37:5). He realizes that the conflicts which characterize the rugged path create doubt in our ability to cope, so He reminds us: "Trust in the Lord with all your heart and do not rely on your own insight" (Proverbs 3:5). He's acquainted with the fact that the conflict with our culture, created by a new and transformed mind, will often put us between the proverbial "rock and a hard place."

So He encourages us: "My grace is sufficient for you, for my power is made perfect in weakness" (2 Corinthians 12:9). Aware of the loneliness which often surrounds the one who whole-heartedly places himself at odds with the world by releasing himself to the will of God, He commits to us: "I am with you always ..." (Matthew 28:20). The paths of leadership formation are engineered by the Father, blazed by His Son, our example, and now, guarded by His Spirit as we follow.

THE PROCESS OF FORMATION

During this particularly difficult and painful time in my ministry, I received a letter of encouragement from my mother, who proceeded to unfold the mysterious blessing and hidden joy of the rugged path. She said it would involve incarnation, then it would lead to Gethsemane, then to Calvary and finally to the Empty Tomb. This path is often the anvil of reality on which a commitment to serve God is hammered out. Human nature tends to avoid it at all cost, because it involves the difficulties of unresolved conflict and misunderstanding. This kind of hurt can only be borne by the soul that has resolved to serve God and minister to people, and it happens only by emptying and humbling self. This is the real incarnation of Jesus. His decision was to serve God's purposes in touching the lives of people by living among them and identifying with them.

This incarnation is necessary in order to become a servant as He was. By it alone we are truly able to overcome the human tendency to callously disregard the needs of others in an attitude of personal superiority. Without following Christ in emptying and humbling ourselves, the needs of people around us will mean little. Those needs will simply become a way we can show how "spiritual" and "kind" we are in "helping the less fortunate." We'll take advantage of others' needs to exalt ourselves. With the removal of all vestiges of personal ambition and defensiveness, we are able to follow Jesus in the step of incarnation. It comes from the compulsion of the compassionate heart of God in us.

After the incarnation there always comes Gethsemane – the temptation (Luke 22:39-42). Here Jesus may have fought His greatest battle. Although the prospect of facing death was horrible, I'm convinced the struggle Jesus faced in Gethsemane was far deeper in nature. I don't think He was trying to get out of dying. Certainly it wasn't a welcome thought, but there was more. Here the forces of self-will and God's will clashed on the battlefield of His life. The temptation to retake control of His destiny was at its greatest intensity. To succumb to that temptation would have aborted the purposes of God and impaired the will of God through Him, since self-will and God's will cannot coexist.

Gethsemane is characterized by the word "choice." It represents that point at which our will rises up to take control in the face of uncertain or unpalatable circumstances. Self-will attempts to do what it wants to do by asserting itself and finding the path of least resistance. Perhaps it would be easier to compromise standards, abandon God's call or take a new position. Those choices might feel preferable to surrendering control. Gethsemane is where the choice to surrender must be made, even though it doesn't make sense to our human nature. In the face of trying circumstances

and accusers, our friends may exhort us to "take control, defend yourself, retaliate, do it your own way," as
if prodding our will to follow its inherently selfish course.
And so the internal battle rages to the point where finally the servant of God makes his or her choice –
"Not my will but Thine be done."

Yet Gethsemane is not the end of the rugged
road. It gets worse. Every choice is tested and requires a
"seal." After Gethsemane there always comes Calvary
(John 19:28-30). Calvary is characterized by the word
"seal." Thinking that temptation was difficult enough,
we are now confronted with crucifixion wherein our
choice is sealed – death to self and life to God. In the
crucifixion the choice to deny self is realized. Not to be
confused with self-denial, denial of self is the willful
replacement of self-mindedness with Christ-mindedness.
At the crucifixion we bring the self-will to be sacrificed
in obedience to God. The choice to surrender is sealed
and self-will is put to death. It no longer exists as a
motivation; personal agenda is erased. Self-ambition is
wiped out. It is no longer able to assert itself with any
kind of coherence.

Indeed, to follow Christ into Gethsemane means
we will, of necessity, follow Him to the testing place of
Calvary. To say with Him, "Not my will but Thine be

done," means that we will of necessity be called upon to say with Him, "Into Thy hands I commend my spirit."

Times come when the white light of truth causes resistance in those who want a less demanding way. When that happens, the incarnational aspect of leadership becomes a crucifixion experience and brings suffering. Still the rugged path is not complete. Although bumps and bruises of hurt and struggle occur on this path, it also carries the promise of God's providence. If we choose to deny self-will in our Gethsemane and allow that choice to be sealed in surrender at Calvary, out of the hurt and denial will come resurrection – new insights, new hope, new visions, new faith, new commitment and new birth.

C.S. Lewis' description of Narnia in his famous *Lion, Witch and the Wardrobe* is memorable. The wicked witch caused it to always be winter and never Christmas. What a hollow condition of despair. No hope. Empty suffering. Much like it would be if there were no resurrection. Imagine the hopelessness if Calvary were the end.

Jesus' final destination was not the cross but the Resurrection. He went through the cross to get to me. Now He's asking me to go through the cross to get to Him.

Even though Calvary always follows
Gethsemane, be encouraged with the knowledge that
after Calvary always comes the empty tomb (1
Corinthians 15:20-22). In the empty tomb is resurrection to newness. This is the result of the "choice" and
the "seal." The choice to surrender in the midst of the
temptation to clutch control, and the crucifying seal of
that choice find result in the full and free activation of
God's will. His will now determines and guides our
activities and agenda. His priorities now steer our
thoughts and mold our mind. The servant now moves
at the impulse of His love and is broken with the things
that break His heart.

Although there may be times in life when we
find ourselves on the rugged path, we cannot abort
God's work in us through it. In my case, I could not
escape the fact that God was not through shaping me
on the rugged path. I saw more clearly than ever that
my identity was rooted in being a servant of God, not
pleasing others (what a release!). Further, to disengage
from the rugged path by accepting a new position in a
safe and cozy environment would have aborted the
leadership formation being done by God. It also would
have betrayed the call at that time in my ministry to
invest myself in other leaders.

It is important to note that Jesus made His own choice to surrender and allowed Himself to undergo the testing of that choice, in faith, believing that the resurrection lay ahead. But it was by the Father's authority that He was raised from the dead. He did not raise Himself; likewise, we do not engineer our own empty tomb. We cannot, in human style, plan exactly how the temptation and crucifixion of the rugged path will unfold into resurrection. Ours is the choice to surrender in faith, believing that the One to whom we surrender will work newness of life in us according to His will and in His time.

Although some who are closest to you may be aware of some dynamic change, little of the rugged path is visible inasmuch as it is primarily a journey in the unseen realm of identity. Who you are is no longer determined by what you do or even by how well you do it. Rather, it is determined by the security found in knowing that you serve God. His will has perfect freedom to be lived out in the function of leadership activities.

Even though the activity of leadership provides the tangible interface with people, as well as the visible circumstances which give opportunity for understanding leadership, the most significant issues are dealt with in the unseen arena of personal identity. Leadership activities are what people will see. The leader is formed in personal identity. Here, as the identity puts on the servant mind of Christ, the foundations of spiritual leadership are established. The top of the "leadership iceberg," then, is given stability and expression.

Chapter

4

THE UPWARD PATH

THE UPWARD PATH

Y ou might be thinking that leadership formation involves only hardship and pain. All this talk about the "downward path" and the " rugged path" might be getting a little discouraging. Why would someone ever willfully choose to endure such experiences? Be encouraged. There is a path leading upward. God will exalt His children. He will bring triumph to those who serve Him. God gives affirmation for those who follow Him on the path to leadership.

A REMINDER

R emember that leadership formation is the shaping of unseen foundations on which our performance will be built and out of which our activities will flow. It is more than simply harmonizing the disciplines of spiritual formation and leadership theory. Leadership formation is the careful and intentional integration of identity and performance, being and doing, essence and activity. What we do in fulfilling our task will be clearly affected and flavored by who we are. Will we be a servant of God and move at His impulses, or will we serve self and pursue our own fulfillment? We cannot compartmentalize who we are from what we are doing any more than we can separate the topside of an iceberg from the lower.

We exist in a performance-oriented culture and operate with a seminar-based learning process. It's what comes naturally to us. In that context, it would be easy to simply engage in more activities in order to balance the two dimensions of leadership – identity and performance. Wrong. That simply becomes another self-motivated effort to do some type of spiritual activity so we can say we're balanced. You may give yourself to all the spiritual disciplines with passion, only to find that it's just another exercise in self-justification. You've missed the point. We don't do balanced activities; we must be balanced people. Leadership formation is a pattern of identity-based becoming. The tasks and activities of leadership, then, will naturally flow from our identity. The performance of our duty will be solidly rooted in an identity that has been forged as a servant of God.

Our goal is not to be or produce arrogant, self-serving, egocentric ladder-climbers. Rather we seek to be and to develop leaders who are confident, competent, emptied and humbled servants of God.

THE PATTERN IN SCRIPTURE

Throughout Scripture, a pattern of formation seems to emerge in the many accounts of God shaping His leaders. This pattern is most clearly articulated in Isaiah 52. Verses 13-15 encapsulate chapters 52-54. They clearly articulate the pattern of formation which is evident in many of the leaders whom God shaped through the course of Old and New Testament history.

The pattern begins with verse 13 defining His leader as a servant. Identity is clearly forged and rooted in servanthood to God. Verse 14 describes the second step of this pattern in terms of "suffering." The servant was marred beyond recognition. Verse 15 describes the exaltation which God brings to His servant. Kings are silenced because of Him. God exalted the one who was clearly identified as His servant and who passed through the suffering to complete exaltation. Among some of the greatest leaders whom God called, this same pattern emerges – identity, suffering, exaltation.

Consider again Philippians 2:5-11 where Jesus Himself represents the pattern on which our leadership is built. He "did not count equality with God a thing to be grasped, but emptied himself, taking the form of a servant." Identity is clearly determined with a release of His position and rights and a commitment of Himself as a servant of His father. Identity is determined as a servant of God. With His identity clearly declared, Jesus entered a stage of suffering. "And being found in human form He humbled Himself and became obedient unto death, even death on a cross." And then note, in verse 11, the final step of the pattern of formation. "God has highly exalted Him ... that at the name of Jesus every knee shall bow ... and every tongue confess that Jesus Christ is Lord, to the glory of God the Father." Thus you see the pattern of formation: identity, suffering and exaltation.

Consider also King David. As a young man, the prophet of God, Samuel, identified and anointed David as king of God's people. David was God's chosen one.

Before God and witnesses, his identity as God's servant was clearly announced and determined.

Yet, how quickly that clarion announcement turned sour. Soon David found himself running from cave to cave as a fugitive, fleeing for his life. His entire lifestyle changed. Can you imagine what was going on in his mind as he scrounged in the desert for food and searched nightly for a place to sleep? After all, he was the anointed king of Israel, yet now he found himself on the run. Imagine the lonely sense of desolation and abandonment which must have been part of his quiet thoughts. *"God, is this all there is? I thought I was to be king. Where did I go wrong? Why is this happening to me, the anointed king!?"* For all David knew, this was the way he would live the rest of his life. At some point he had to come to grips with the possibility that this was his destiny.

Following the same pattern of formation, David found himself exalted to the point of being king and even being called "a man after God's own heart." Through him deliverance would come to God's people. Confidence in leading a nation had been forged on the anvil of suffering and rooted in his identity as a servant of God. First there was a declaration of identity, next a process of suffering and finally the exaltation came.

Consider also, the embellished story of Moses in the prologue and epilogue of this book. He was a man well-bred in the courts of Pharaoh. He was clearly marked as a future leader of his people. Moses had received opportunities to observe leaders in action and to be trained with the skills necessary for competent and high-performance tasks. The moment he began to wield his abilities, however, he found himself face-to-face with the desolate and lonely well which marked the beginning of his wilderness journey. Without doubt, intense suffering in his inner thoughts and emotions accompanied the mundane task of shepherding sheep. Reconciling his lonely and lowly position alone in the desert with what he knew to be his training and up-bringing as a leader must have created an intense struggle within his soul. For all he knew, this was to be how he would live the rest of his life. Through this process, Moses had to come to the point where he accepted the possibility that this was his destiny.

The pattern of formation again emerges in its final step of exaltation. Moses found himself face-to-face with God Who raised him to lead His people and bestowed upon him the glory of His presence as none other had ever known. Through him deliverance would come to God's people. Confidence as a leader had been forged in Moses on the anvil of suffering. Through the lonely years in the wilderness he had experienced self-doubt, uncertainty and searching as God brought him face-to-face with the core of his identity. All he did in leading the people was now rooted in identity as a servant of God.

This pattern of leadership formation seems to appear in case after case throughout Scripture. There is a clear statement of identity as a servant, with a subsequent process of suffering and breaking. Finally, there is exaltation and powerful leadership. This pattern is not merely another exercise in activities. I am convinced that we cannot fully understand it outside of personal experience. It cannot be dissected and analyzed in a purely academic investigation. To do so relegates the scriptural pattern of leadership formation to being merely another activity that can be learned at a seminar or event. Don't expect a five-step manual of what you can do to experience this pattern of formation. This is the pattern through which God guides His leaders in leadership formation for effective service to Him. He does it in His time and in His way.

In each case throughout the Bible, these three steps always seem to be present. We might wonder if there is any chance of moving directly from a clear statement of identity to exaltation. Unfortunately it is not possible. Exaltation without suffering becomes the exaltation of self. It is through the wilderness journeying – times of loneliness, searching, self-doubt and often pain – that release of self-reliance occurs. Through this process the core of our identity is rewired. Self is no longer at the center. The subsequent exaltation, then, is not of self but of God and His will.

THE PATTERN IS DESCRIPTIVE

When it comes to understanding how this pattern is "fleshed out," there's an important point I need to make. In our contemporary Christian culture, we have a tendency to diagnose a problem and then prescribe a solution or cure. Invariably, we not only approach church issues this way but also tend to think of our own development with this prescriptive mindset. We may assume that this pattern of formation can be prescriptive in nature. That is to say that we may attempt to engineer ourselves or others through the steps of becoming a spiritual leader. In an over-aggressive effort to be what we think God wants us to be, we may seek painful circumstances or at least wallow in suffering by adopting a martyr attitude. We glorify the suffering process assuming that this only makes us more spiritual and potentially more effective.

In actual fact, Isaiah 52:14 represents a parenthetical statement which is "descriptive" in nature. Suffering is a parenthesis between the clear statement of who we are in our identity and the exalted role which God gives as His leader. Suffering is neither to become an end in itself, nor does it serve a virtuous purpose of its own. It is not to be engineered or sought after. It's simply part of the pattern of leadership formation in becoming a servant of God.

We do not intentionally prescribe circumstances and situations by which this pattern of formation becomes a part of our life. We simply acknowledge that these will be part of the shaping of who we are, once we have committed ourselves to being His servant. Expect it. Recognize it. Accept it. And understand its possible impact on you. In any case, always maintain an attitude of open submission to God's work in forming your identity. That's not easy to do. Our instinct is self-defense, self-justification and self-affirmation. Remember, though, it is your "self" God is seeking to replace. So the natural defense mechanisms will only prevent the rewiring God seeks to do in shaping your identity as His servant.

Recently, I was asked if this pattern of formation may look different in each of us based on our different personalities. In other words, does an emotionally oriented individual have the same ability to comprehend this pattern of leadership formation as one who is more logically driven? That's a good question which perhaps experience alone can answer. To resolve that question would require comprehensive and personal experience with all personalities. I am not sure that anyone can exhaustively do that.

One obvious thing, however, is that every person, regardless of personality type or style, ultimately must come to a point where they recognize the pattern of formation which God is using to shape them as His servant. By whatever means you may come to that recognition, it will become evident as the foundation of your identity.

For you, it may be on more affective, emotional and less analytical terms. For your friend, it may be through a logical progression of events. It may be extremely well-defined, with clear points of experience separating the steps in the process. Or perhaps it will feel as though all three of these – identity, suffering, exaltation – are superimposed on each other, all happening at once. That's OK. You're unique. Don't look for the same process God has used in me or your friend. Just look for the truth of God and His hand at work shaping you as He wills.

Chapter

5

THE
BROADENING
PATH

THE ROLE OF FOUNDATIONS

While living in Dallas, I frequently traveled to the downtown area for appointments or meetings. On one occasion, as I walked from my car to the office where my meeting was to be held, I passed the construction site for one of the skyscrapers which now dominates the Dallas skyline. The city was exploding with growth, so construction sites like this were not uncommon. On this particular day, however, I noticed that one of the sheets of plywood which surrounded the site was missing. This afforded me an unobstructed view of the entire scene. It happened that this building was in the early stages. What I saw was a huge hole in the ground. I looked in amazement at how deep and wide the hole was. The builders were going down to secure a broad foundation before they could go up with the superstructure.

Similarly, the broadening path takes us to the foundation from which we discover the breadth and possibilities of leadership. Every leader has a foundation for his or her leadership. Leadership cannot exist without a foundation any more than a building can stand without one. The question is, "What kind of foundation is it?" Ultimately, the foundation will determine the breadth and nature of our leadership.

When I say "foundation," I'm not referring to some type of introduction or orientation. Perhaps you recall taking a foundations class in school. Usually it implied that the material covered was introductory in nature, a survey or orientation class to whet the appetite. Here, however, I use the term "foundation" to describe the basis or footings on which leadership is built.

This kind of foundation is extremely important and requires careful attention. It can create coherence, unity and strength in our leadership, or it can cause division, inconsistency and weakness.

Consider the concept of being "unequally yoked together" as we read in Scripture. We understand it as a principle to be applied to marriage relationships. You may teach your children that it's not wise to marry someone who's not a Christian. "Why?" they ask. "We both like basketball, Italian food, jazz, hiking and Star Trek. We have so many things in common. We're made for each other." Wisely you attempt to help them realize that there is more to life than sports, leisure and vocation. There are basic foundations that guide us. The foundation on which our common interests rest must also be compatible.

A few years later, that child may return and say, "You were right. I tried to make it work. For a while it did. We enjoyed so much together. But the deeper we probed in our relationship the greater the differences became. Soon we realized that our priorities were different. Our motivations were different. Our foundations were different."

Now apply that principle to leadership. We import styles and theories from the secular workplace. We assume that what works out there will work in the church. After a while, we may pick up on subtle conflicts which begin to creep into our thinking. As we embrace an imported pattern of leadership, we may begin to sense greater discomfort on a spiritual level. Or else we may find ourselves compromising values or priorities in order to reconcile our leadership activities with who we are. Increasingly, our identity creates conflict with a pattern of leadership which may be built on a different foundation. This is "unequally yoked."

That's not to say that we toss leadership lessons from IBM and Xerox out the window. There's a great deal we can learn from them. But we must realize that the foundational motivations are different. "How?" you ask. Stay with me for the next few pages and I think you'll see it.

I would like to show you the contrast between a secular foundation for leadership and a spiritual foundation. By doing so in general terms, the goal is to make the point, not to treat the related issues exhaustively. Understand, also, that this same pattern goes beyond leadership issues to describe healthy foundations of spiritual life which give rise to a healthy Christian lifestyle. There's a priority lesson here for Christians in general. Especially now, in the face of pervasive dysfunctional behavior among church members in a contemporary generation which is obsessed with "top of the iceberg" behavior.

Let me start with a cursory description of various theories and patterns that exist in the business and educational organizations around us. We'll proceed to the foundation on which much of those patterns are built, construct a new spiritual foundation and then add back the leadership activities. Visually our discussion might look like this:

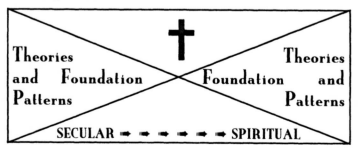

Perhaps you've had opportunity to become acquainted with leadership styles and management theory through courses at school or in your personal reading. If so, our discussion here will simply serve to remind you. If not, it will be just enough to help you get a general idea. You can read other books to get a complete understanding of what we touch on here.

LEADERSHIP THEORIES

Modern organizational studies in the '30s, including the famous Hawthorne studies, began to examine the various factors affecting people in the workplace. This was the start of industrial and organizational psychology and various theories of management.

Theory X generally holds that the task is the highest priority for the leader. Leadership is task-oriented and tends to be autocratic in nature. The task is highly directed by the leader who believes that people require high control. This theory assumes that people will avoid work and need coercion; basically, they are lazy. It further assumes that work is distasteful, and motivation to work will only happen at the physical or safety level in the worker.

Theory Y, on the other hand, is behavior-oriented. Developed by Douglas McGregor, it is people-centered and democratic in nature. Creativity is encouraged. Motivation occurs within the worker at the social, esteem and self-actualization levels.

Theory Z, articulated by Japanese management leader Ouchi, defines leadership as participatory. Decisions are made with input from all involved in a participative process. Evaluation is a critical component and the feedback loop is essential for effective leadership.

Another theory Z was defined by Henry Sisk at North Texas State University. Sisk basically combines theories X and Y in a hybrid theory that he calls "contingency management." In other words, the style of leadership used will be contingent on the circumstances faced by the leader. This demands analysis skills in balancing the human needs of workers with the need to fulfill the task at hand.

LEADERSHIP STYLES

You may also remember how we generally describe four different styles of applying leadership. While these may be adjusted according to the situation, the leader's personality is probably more of a determining factor in selecting which one will be used.

The autocratic style of leadership usually proceeds from the task-oriented theory X. It places focus upon fulfilling the task, sometimes at the expense of the people involved. On the other hand, a democratic style places higher value on the role of people and often flows from theory Y. Although it may require more time to fulfill the task, people will feel involved. Further, the leader must accept the reality that the democratic process will produce a result with compromises.

The laissez-faire leader most probably operates from theory Y. Allowing that assumption, however, may be too generous. This style simply manages what's there. The manager merely allows things to take their own course with little influence. It may even be difficult to justify this as a leadership style since little leadership actually occurs.

Participatory leadership is closely connected to the Z theories. It involves people to the degree and at the level the leader believes will help the worker produce the best results. The emphasis remains on the task, but with the recognition that workers who are involved in the process will produce better results.

Al Guskin has similarly categorized styles of leadership using terms that are perhaps less laden or stereotypical. The "heroic" leader is characterized by "I" and leads from a charismatic position. Information flow is downward and delegation is limited. Dependence on formal authority and position is great.

The "mediator" is characterized by "You" and focuses on the elimination of adversarial roles. Delegation of authority is a principal activity. Decisions are made largely as a result of external factors.

The "team" leader is characterized by "Us" and is that style wherein building the team is the major issue. The process of decision-making is as important as the decision itself. This leader is collaborative not assertive. The organization is built on interpersonal sensitivity.

Another contribution of the secular business and management world is the development of grids to aid in assessing leadership styles and management conditions. A couple of the better known include one developed by Robert Blake and Jane Mouton, and one by Robert Tannenbaum and Warren Schmidt.

Blake and Mouton use the people/product dichotomy and orient them on an X and Y axis. On a scale from 1 to 9 the management style of the leader is charted on each axis. To what degree do they show concern for people or concern for product or task? The result is a general description of the leader's style in balancing or integrating the two.

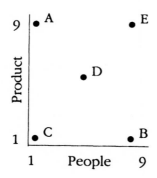

A 9-1   is product-oriented using high authority and demanding high obedience.

B 1-9   is people-oriented using a "country club" style of pleasing people.

C 1-1   is a non-directional and impoverished condition of no leadership.

D 5-5   is organizational in nature and seeks to please the majority and appease the minority.

E 9-9   is team-oriented with people involved in the task.

Tannenbaum and Schmidt also use polar terms as the basis for their grid. In their case, however, the contrasting extremes are the manager and the subordinate. To what degree is the leader centered on his or her own objectives? To what degree does the leader seek to develop or empower subordinates? The farther to the extremes a leader is placed on the grid, the less successful he or she is at balancing both for a healthy and effective organization.

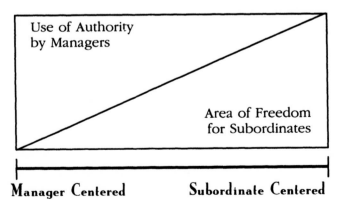

Use of Authority by Managers

Area of Freedom for Subordinates

Manager Centered   Subordinate Centered

You might say, "This is nice, somewhat informative and even a bit fun to play with in my coffeebreak conversations. But what in the world does it have to do with leadership formation with the mind of Christ?" Stick with me and let's turn a corner.

A SECULAR FOUNDATION

Leadership styles, theories and grids can be wonderful contributions to Christian leaders. They can serve to sharpen, focus and equip us. The question is, "What is the foundation undergirding these and from which they proceed?" The most effective use of these patterns of leadership by Christian leaders can only come after we've examined the motivational foundation. We have to ensure that as we broaden our leadership horizons by learning from these patterns, we are doing so on a sound foundation that is consistent with the nature of the church, our calling and the mind of Christ. Anything less may create conflict with the organismic nature of the church and God's work in us.

So what is the foundation of these theories and styles? A good case can be made that one of the most significant sources of motivation for many of these and other theories lies in the early 20th century ideas of Abraham Maslow. Specifically I refer to his Hierarchy of Human Needs.

Neither time nor space allow us to treat Maslow and his hierarchy exhaustively. Simply put, however, the Hierarchy of Human Needs identified what Maslow felt were the basic and ascending needs of every person. These five levels of human needs served as the source of motivation for human activity – whether job related, personal or relational.

At the first and basic level, according to Maslow, every person acts out of a motivation to meet physical needs. This is the survival instinct that exists in every person. Once this need is met, people begin to be motivated by a need for safety. Amid the threats and insecurities of life, security becomes the primary concern after basic survival is assured. You might recall my earlier statement that the theory X, or task-oriented environment, assumes that people are motivated at one of these levels.

After the physical and safety needs are met, people begin to recognize the need for social interaction. A powerful urge to belong motivates involvement in groups and sub-groups. Perhaps it's the Lions Club, PTA, church or a bowling league. Everyone experiences a need to belong once basic physical and safety needs have been resolved.

Next on the list of needs is esteem. Now that a person belongs to a group, he or she needs to be acknowledged as a contributing member. People need recognition for their accomplishments. This gives them a sense of esteem. Self-worth is significantly affected by this recognition. And here you can begin to see subtle conflicts percolating up in the life of a person or leader who operates on this foundation. Recognition for personal accomplishments is certainly important, but it may not be the healthiest source of esteem and self-worth for a Christian. This will become clearer shortly.

Ultimately, in the Hierarchy of Human Needs, every person has a need to be self-actualized. This self-actualization involves complete and holistic fulfillment of our individual potential on a constantly growing basis. Here people are operating in a well-balanced manner at full level of capacity.

This hierarchy, and particularly its goal of self-actualization, has become the basis for the student development movement on modern college campuses. If the ultimate goal of the university is to facilitate self-actualization as a means to producing holistic students, then student development was designed to marshal the institutional resources to that end.

Obviously, such a brief description can't possibly do justice to the complexities of the self-actualization of human potential. It involves the development of people physically, emotionally, intellectually, socially and, yes, even spiritually. Yet for all the effort to include a spiritual dimension, it still remains one component of the larger goal to actualize the self. On this foundation, a person's primary motivation results from a desire for self-improvement. No matter how hard you may try to spiritualize or adapt the foundation to a Christian context, "self" remains at the apex – the ultimate goal and master.

Self-Actualization

Esteem

Social

Safety

Physical

Hierarchy of Human Needs

(Motivation results from a desire for self-improvement.)

This foundation of self-actualization has become the basis and motivation for many of the styles, patterns and theories we touched on previously. The desire to be self-actualized motivates much of our human activity. Because it is so prevalent in secular activities, and because we often import those activities into the church, we can easily create potential conflict at the foundational level if we don't rewire our foundation. Actualization of "self" is not an appropriate foundation or motivation for your leadership in the church. The foundation requires a complete overhaul.

A NEW FOUNDATION

Consider an alternate foundation, one that is rewired, built upon scriptural principles – a new foundation which provides coherence and integration with the organismic nature of the body of Christ. One which is overhauled and allows complete integrity between who we are and the leadership patterns and styles we use.

For purposes of communication, imagine if Abraham Maslow had been converted – reborn, committed to Christ. I know there are many who say that in his latter years he acknowledged the spiritual dimension within human beings. But what if that dimension were part of his hierarchy? Adding a spiritual dimension to the concept of self-actualization is nothing more than spiritualizing the self. A truly new foundation needs to be built fresh from the ground up. Perhaps it would look something like this.

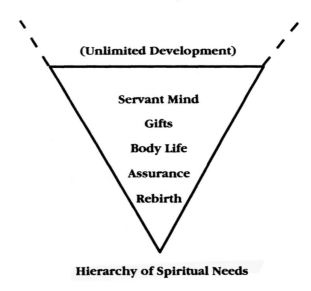

Hierarchy of Spiritual Needs

(Motivation results from a passion for God.)

On this new hierarchy of spiritual needs there is first a need to be reborn. Like Nicodemus, each of us must come to a point of decision wherein we choose to reject or accept new life in Christ. We are born anew into the kingdom of God. Accepting the work of Jesus and the merit of His sacrifice, we join His family as fellow heirs (Romans 10:9).

After you lead a person to saving faith in Christ, what's the first major question he or she asks you? "How do I know I am a child of God?" In new Christians there's a high need for assurance. Doubts begin to crowd their thinking soon after a decision to follow Christ. If you lead them to that decision, you must now help them develop an inner assurance of sins forgiven (1 John 5:13-14).

Quickly, then, they begin to sense a need to be part of a larger group. Body life becomes a driving need. Especially in newer Christians, this need to be with others can hardly be fully satisfied. Any time the church is open, they're there. They can't get enough Christian fellowship. Belonging is an elemental need for every Christian, new or old (1 Corinthians 12:12).

Once Christians are fairly secure in faith and belonging, they might soon begin to ask about ministry opportunities. "How can I help? Can I teach Sunday school? Can I plan an event?" They are being motivated by the need to be active in ministry through the use of gifts. This is a critical transition point which many Christians never make. Many assume that body life is enough. Church attendance and relationships are sufficient. They may never press on to active ministry in their gifts. In many cases they become stagnant in their spiritual life. With no outflow of ministry, they can be likened to the Dead Sea – a body of water with little life.

A healthy understanding of all the gifts of the Spirit and effective use of particular gifts is what marks a maturing Christian. In Scripture this point is a significant one (Ephesians 4:11-12).

Mature Christians, effectively using their gifts and experiencing consistent growth in their faith, may be motivated further in their journey by a need to put on the servant mind of Christ. This is the one who is emptied for service and humbled in obedience to God. This requires active surrender by our human will as I've already described in Chapter 2 (Philippians 2:5-7).

Just as some people never move to the level of self-actualization on the Hierarchy of Human Needs, there are also Christians who never understand or adopt the servant mind on the Hierarchy of Spiritual Needs. It exists, however, as a powerful need which motivates Christian leaders and which can only be met in God.

Look back at the Hierarchy of Human Needs. Notice how the triangle comes to a point at the top. Self-actualization is the apex, the top, the limit. But it is also limited. Arriving at self-actualization, persons find themselves in a limited "corner." Any theory or pattern of leadership built on this foundation will be inherently limited due to the finite nature of mankind and the commensurate limits of self-actualization.

Now look at the Hierarchy of Spiritual Needs. Notice that when the lines of the triangle are projected upward, they never meet to form a corner. There is unlimited potential since the identity is rooted in God, Who is infinite. He is unfathomable and therefore our identity and relationship in Him are likewise limitless.

The key difference between these two foundations is the source of motivation. In one, motivation results from a desire for self-improvement. In the other, motivation results from a passion for God.

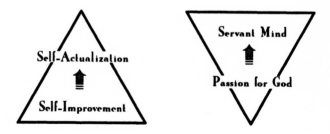

Any attempt to include a spiritual dimension in the process of self-actualization is merely that – an attempt. Self always remains at the apex. It remains at the center of motivation and activity. It remains the god to be served.

The pastor at our home church recently made the point this way. "If you devote yourself to self, guess what you get? Right. You! If you devote yourself to God, guess what you get? God." There are many religious activities and leadership theories which are built on the motivation for self-improvement. In every case self remains central and foundational. Within the church only activities and patterns built on a new foundation will maintain integrity with its spiritual nature.

With a new foundation, a rewired core and a transformed identity, the layers of activities, styles and patterns can be put back in place. Only now, they proceed from a different foundation. Now, with secure footings, our leadership activities can broaden with the assurance of a healthy foundation that is compatible with the spiritual environment in which we operate. We may use some of the same theories we've discussed before. Only now there is greater breadth and a different motivation. Our passion for God drives us to learn everything we can to be more effective as leaders.

With a new foundation, we can be freed from the need to constantly defend self. Time need not be wasted on learning how to manipulate the environment in order to exalt self. Insecurities about our identity can give way to a holy boldness which pursues God and His truth. We don't have to spend time and energy propping up our identity with activity, or worse yet, redefining success in order to justify ourselves.

When self is the motivating center of who we are, we will do everything possible to defend it, exalt it and promote it even if that means reframing our circumstances. If my primary motivation is to improve myself through performance, and my performance isn't too good, I have a problem. Rather than let my identity be crushed, I'll simply rationalize my performance and twist it somehow to make it look good. That way I'm protecting myself from being hurt.

In putting on the servant mind of Christ, however, our motivation is not to exalt or improve self, but rather, it is a passion for God. The core of our identity is no longer rooted in self but in God. When attacks come from circumstances or disagreeable people, the target they're aiming at is not there. Ego is gone. It's replaced by a new master – God. The arrows shot at us may hurt, but they miss their intended target – our self-based identity – since it has been replaced. If we are a servant of self and self is attacked, it may crush our identity. If we are a servant of God and we are attacked, our identity remains undamaged.

While there may be valuable truths in our critics' words from which we should learn, we stand whole, because our new identity is secure. We can listen to the criticism, sift through it, and accept what is truth – and there's always some truth to be found.

The two foundations I've described each have a highest need. In one, it is self-actualization. In the other, that highest need is the servant mind. Let's contrast the two a bit more explicitly.

SELF-ACTUALIZATION	SERVANT MIND
Fulfillment of human potential	Fulfillment of God's potential in us
Achieved by increased control	Achieved by released control
Centered on self	Centered on God
Focused on self-rights	Focused on ministry to others
Act of the will is to do better and more	Act of the will is to surrender

Constructing a new foundation for our leadership activities is not easy or quick. It takes time, commitment and submission. In a day when we operate with a "microwave" mentality, we may assume we can simply "pop something in" and it'll be "done" in no time. Still, there are things which only "come out" properly after time and care in a "convection" oven.

This process may be slow and require perseverance and care. It isn't quick. And there will be times when our self-will may attempt to "rise up" and retake center stage and control. Remember that self-actualization, as we've discussed it here, and the servant mind of Christ are mutually exclusive. They cannot coexist. That which obsesses our mind, heart and motivation will direct our lives and leadership.

On the broadening path, we use any leadership theories and techniques we can to fulfill our call. But they are given greater breadth of effectiveness by being built on a new foundation. It not only provides greater freedom from self, but that new foundation is also compatible with the spiritual, organismic nature of the church.

Chapter

6

THE
OUTWARD
PATH

THE OUTWARD PATH

I'd like to turn a corner. If you're anything like me, there always comes a point when you begin to get fidgety to "do" something. Truths like these must have a pragmatic application. If not, what good are they?

INTEGRATING IDENTITY AND ACTIVITY

Do you remember our analogy of the iceberg? Let's extend it a bit further – the analogy, that is, not the iceberg. An iceberg is a mountain of frozen fresh water. We all know that the seas in which they float are salt water. Thus, icebergs are "in the sea" but not "of the sea." Their character and nature are different than their surrounding environment.

As a Christian leader pursuing the mind of Christ, your character and nature are different than the surrounding environment. Your foundation is different; your motivation is different. Your identity is changed. You are "in the world" but not "of the world." There must be a reason.

Consider further that every iceberg has a visible part and a non-visible part. I've never heard of an iceberg that only exists beneath the waterline. Always a portion sticks up out of the water into public view. It may be small, but it's always there.

The outward path of leadership formation leads us to understand and embrace the reason why a new foundation is so important; why a rewired identity is so critical to us as Christian leaders; why we are "in the world" but not "of the world." This path moves us outward into the public realm of the visible activities which flow from a servant mind.

If we have put on the servant mind of Christ (Philippians 2:5), our identity is clearly defined as a servant of God. But as I've explained already, it doesn't stop there. Christ became a servant to His Father for a reason. It was to fulfill His Father's task. The Father's agenda, passion and mission became His. The Father's mission was to reconcile His creation back to Himself. That became Christ's mission.

Fallen humanity's greatest need is to be reconciled to God. Out of His passion for His creation, God made a way for that to happen – through faith in Christ. In a supreme act of servanthood, Christ obeyed His Father, submitted Himself and made that possible.

In like-mindedness Christian leaders follow His example – obey the Father, submit to His will and make Christ known as the means for reconciliation to God. That's our ministry. Not ours personally, but ours because it's God's and we are His servants. Ministering to the needs of people – the greatest of which is reconciliation – is God's passion at work through us, because we are His servants.

Jesus came to serve God and minister to people. On the outward path that truth comes full circle. We minister to the needs of people as an expression of our commitment to serve God. Our identity finds expression in activity. The activity of ministry flows from identity as a servant. A servant of God, fully surrendered to His agenda and priority, will be compelled to minister to people.

Isaiah was transformed in his character and nature by God Himself. He was compelled to "go" in response to the call of God (Isaiah 6:1-8). When you follow the paths of leadership formation, it will include the outward path. You will be compelled to "go" in ministry to people. That's God's agenda and priority at work through one of His servants.

In 1 Peter 2:9, perhaps the clearest scriptural explanation of this integration of our identity and our activity is given. We are "a chosen race, a royal priesthood, a holy nation, God's own people. ..." This describes our identity, who we are, and has to do with being, essence, nature. This is the bottom of the iceberg. But these things are true for a reason. We are who we are for a purpose.

The second half of the verse turns us outward. It moves us to the top of the iceberg. We are God's people "in order that ..." – here comes task, activity, mission, doing – "we may make known the wonderful deeds of Him who called us out of darkness into His marvelous light."

Do you see it? Identity flows into activity, and activity is built upon identity. Who we are compels us to action in ministry. We serve God in order to minister to people.

THE CENTER POINT

Our identity as a servant of God is the center point around which our activity in ministry revolves. Because it is rooted in God, it does not move, vacillate or change with various circumstances. Our anchored center point is our identity as a servant of God.

Without an intentional, willful commitment to be a servant of God, you will be serving self and other people. In either case they are relative, changing, fickle and always moving.

Upon finishing my college work six months early, I decided I'd stay in the area and wait to begin graduate studies. That way I could move on at the same time as my classmates. Many of us were planning to attend the same graduate school. So I hung around western New York and did a few things I'd always wanted to do. One of those things was learning to fly.

One day, early in the process, we flew to the practice area and my instructor informed me we'd be doing "turns about a point." The idea was to select a fixed point on the ground and fly a perfect circle around that point, keeping the aircraft at an equal distance all the way around. The pilot has to compensate for wind always keeping the same distance from the fixed point.

My instructor selected a barn and proceeded to demonstrate the exercise. Then he said, "Now it's your turn. You have the airplane. First, pick a point on the ground." I looked around on the ground and finally said, "How 'bout that cow down there?" Needless to say we had a pretty good laugh at the thought of that cow meandering all over the pasture pleasing its stomach while I flew like a crazy man trying to keep circling it.

Is your center point fixed and immovable? Or is it relative and changing? Do you serve God, or do you serve self and people? All your ministry activities will revolve around your center point. If it's fixed, there will be coherence, order and effectiveness in your ministry activities. If not, you'll soon be exhausted trying to serve yourself and people who move all over the landscape with expectations for you to keep "circling" them.

SELF-AWARENESS

The leader, whose identity is unequivocally rooted as a servant of God, will have greater ability to develop the essential leadership quality of self-awareness. Self-awareness is the ability to evaluate your leadership role objectively. If self is at the center of your leadership, that will be a difficult, if not impossible, exercise. If self has been surrendered, evaluating your leadership will not pose a threat. Once you lose self-awareness, leadership effectiveness is severely hampered.

I apply the quality of self-awareness to two leadership arenas. In the personal arena, self-awareness means continually evaluating the integration and interaction between our identity and our performance. In other words, it's a regular awareness of the integrated relationship between the bottom and top of the iceberg – who we are and what we do. Lack of awareness of this dynamic relationship reduces the power of your leadership significantly. Furthermore, it causes you to revert to a compartmentalized view of spiritual formation and leadership development. Usually the result is that you will approach everything, including your spiritual formation, as simply another discipline to be studied and learned through skill acquisition.

The second arena to which I apply the quality of self-awareness is what I call the positional arena. By this I mean the particular position you as a leader have in a specific context. What is the level of effectiveness in influence, operation and presence which you have in a particular situation? That situation includes the variables of people, resources, history and potential. What is the "chemistry" of your relationship with your context? If you are not always aware and evaluating that dynamic mix, your effectiveness is limited as a leader.

In both arenas, the servant of self is severely handicapped. He or she is not only concerned about fulfilling a task, but also doing it in a way that protects and even exalts self. The servant of God is freed for higher and broader effectiveness.

As a leader, operating with the servant mind of Christ and employing the quality of self-awareness, you are uniquely entrusted by God with responsibility to lead. This kind of leadership calling will transcend specific positions of leadership. It becomes a channel or vehicle through which you are empowered by God to lead in various contexts. This kind of leadership does not derive its effectiveness from the position or field you're in. It's like a shell which can be applied to numerous circumstances.

You may, for a season, be a pastor; then you may apply your leadership calling to the field of education. Or perhaps you lead in a secular business, then you may assume a position as an ambassador where your leadership, built on the same principles, is equally effective. I'm not saying that this pattern of Christian leadership qualifies you for all these positions, only that leadership on these principles is not tied to a single application.

LEADERSHIP RESPONSIBILITIES

No matter what context you find yourself in right now, your leadership activity can proceed from an identity clearly forged as a servant of God. Flowing from that identity, your responsibility is basically threefold – cast vision, create environment and lead your people.

In casting vision you become like the eye piece on a telescope. When you point a telescope to the stars, many lenses capture the light, bend it, refract it and magnify it. But it's the eye piece which puts the magnified light into final focus. It sharpens the image, defines the shape and gives the light meaning. You may have the largest telescope in the world but remove the eye piece, and all you're doing is bending light.

Likewise, you may have a talented group of people around you, great facilities, wonderful programs, refined systems and plenty of money. But without a servant leader, there is no vision and without vision, the organism dies. You are the leader – the eye piece. You put the vision in focus. Whether you influence a church, a business, a university or a friend, it is your identity expressing itself in activity that provides vision, and therein is life.

In creating environment, you are affecting the atmosphere around you to be more conducive to the vision. Again, as in vision casting, it is your identity as a servant of God which will flow into the environment you influence. If your identity is self-centered, you'll find an environment that is self-centered, defensive, territorial and hostile. Conversely, transparency, vulnerability, trust and openness tend to proceed from a leader who is emptied and humbled before God.

Furthermore, if you take the same relationship between identity and activity within an individual and apply it on a corporate level, the same dynamic occurs. An environment characterized by a servant mind – motivated by a passion for God, emptied for service, humbled in obedience – will naturally give rise to activities and systems that are consistent with God's heart. Once again, on a corporate level, activities are motivated by the One whom we serve. We are compelled to do corporately the things that are important to our Master.

That's the point at which leading the people becomes a responsibility. Remember your third general responsibility as a Christian leader. In managing organizational resources – facilities, funds, people – you have a responsibility to ensure that the activities are consistent with the identity. Sometimes that means resourcing people. Other times it involves guiding, disciplining or protecting. Whatever is required, you lead your organization or group in fulfilling the specific mission, while maintaining integrity with the corporate identity and nature.

The outward path begins to take us out of the unseen realm into the public domain of performance. It helps us to understand the close relationship between who we are and what we do. While another volume may be required to explore visible leadership activities which flow from a servant mind, the point here is to recognize that they are intertwined. They cannot be separated. Activity flows from identity. Our identity informs and defines the nature of our visible leadership activities. For the servant of God, this means we are propelled by who we are into doing what will fulfill our Master's mission.

CONCLUSION

A few years ago our family decided to invite our close friends to join us on a brief, five-day vacation to the Grand Canyon. Each family traveled in a van, and we always stayed together, caravan style. At meal times or scenic stops on the journey we would excitedly talk about the beautiful vistas along the way. Interestingly, we discovered that, although we had traveled the same road under similar circumstances and even looked at the same scenery, we saw and experienced different things. The journey was unique for each of us. The paths were the same, but the journey was personal.

Don't expect your journey on the paths of leadership formation to be exactly like another's. The pattern may be the same, the effect may be similar, but the journey is unique.

Furthermore, don't expect your friend or associate to experience exactly what you've experienced. Imposing your particular journey on another person can abort the very work God and you may desire in him or her. Recognize the principles at work. See the patterns. Look for the effect, but allow God to make the paths of their journey unique.

Spiritual leaders demonstrate characteristics which will be obvious no matter what the circumstances of their personal journey. Look for a broken heart. You can see the pain of that brokenness if you look closely enough. It's usually wrapped in victorious joy, a peace that passes human understanding. If you're beginning your journey, follow the leader who walks with a limp. He or she has been where you must go.

Look for a servant mind. Not simply a lifestyle that does "service" activities, but a mind that is transformed. One that is clearly in conflict with natural, human, self-centered tendencies. One that is humble and holy with the nature of God Himself. He or she manifests the pattern you seek.

Look for a release of rights. A life that grasps tightly to any self rights is not fully surrendered and cannot show you the paths of formation. In order for a leader to be truly formed after the pattern of Christ, personal rights have to be released. This leader holds loosely to position, power and personal agenda. He or she will model the lifestyle that must be adopted.

The call of God to leadership always seems to include the appearance of God in fresh vision, our personal hesitation and reluctance, God's transforming touch, and a task given by Him. In responding, our character is transformed; the result is healthy and whole ministry. It doesn't happen unless we choose for it to happen. We must willfully commit to the journey of leadership formation.

The journey of formation begins on the downward path. It continues to the rugged path, on the upward path, then on the broadening path. Finally it takes us on the outward path where it impacts people, organizations and movements. This is where ministry can truly begin. When we choose to follow Christ in His incarnation, we will find ourselves following Him in formation and ultimately in continuing His ministry.

When you follow the pattern of Christ, integration between the bottom of the iceberg and the top begins to occur within you.

Being leads to doing

Identity leads to activity

Purpose leads to mission

Loving God leads to loving people

Being holy leads to making disciples

Knowing God leads to making Him known

Entering His presence leads to going into the world

God will not change your circumstances until He first changes you. Then you will be in a condition to be His servant, His instrument, His vessel by which you may alter your environment on His agenda. You see, leadership starts with servanthood – to God.

My prayer for you is that you will choose to serve God and follow Him on the journey of leadership formation; that you will remain soft on the paths where He will guide you; that you will be emptied and humbled for Him; that you will embrace the circumstances and experiences by which God will help you in becoming a servant of God.

GOD BE WITH YOU.

EPILOGUE

THE BUSH

The faint flash of light in the distance caught his attention. He looked, but couldn't see where it had come from. Turning once again to the task at hand of shepherding, he noticed the glimmer again out of the corner of his eye. He decided to move his flock in that direction to see if he could discover what it was. As he drew closer, he could look directly at the source and see that it was some kind of light. In this barren territory it could only mean that someone was nearby. As lonely as it got in the wilderness, Moses welcomed the thought of companionship to break the monotony of the day.

He could detect that it was a fire of some sort, but he could see no humans anywhere. He knew that fires didn't just start by themselves, and he sensed a mixture of concern, curiosity and fear welling up within him. He walked on ahead of his flock, knowing they would remain within sight and would not grow agitated.

As he drew closer to the fire, a strange puzzlement began to creep over him. He saw a fire, but no sign of people or a camp. A vaguely familiar spark of energy from some mysterious source drove him faster to the site of this burning bush. He'd seen a lot of things in this wilderness and learned a great deal over 40 years of routine shepherding, but he'd never come across anything like this before. A bush that was burning and no one around who could have started it. How strange. Even stranger was the fact that the fire seemed to be growing no dimmer. It was not going out – the bush was not burning, and yet it was. Something told Moses that this was no ordinary bush, no ordinary fire.

He was now at the site of the burning bush. His senses told him to go no further and not to attempt to touch it. He simply stood in the presence of this unusual sight. Filled with exhilaration, fear, awe and attraction, he soaked in the deep, warming peace and confidence which seemed to emanate from the bush and overwhelm his being with a depth and thoroughness he never thought possible.

What was happening to him? He was experiencing depths within him he never knew existed, and yet he knew it was by no intention of his own. He had spent countless hours wandering the paths of this wilderness communing with and sometimes struggling with God. Could it be that this God whom he had sought in times of deep despair, this God whom he had praised in moments of indescribable joy was revealing Himself in a new, all-consuming way? That had to be it. But why now? Why here? What had caused this?

After what seemed an eternity, those questions seemed to dissolve when the unmistakable presence of God's holiness overwhelmed him. The message was clear. "Take off your shoes, you are standing on holy ground." His heart leaped. His mind whirled. He was in the presence of God! The awful, overwhelming, penetrating, transforming presence of the Holy One.

Over the next few moments he felt his life changing as never before. The very root of his nature was purged and ignited. The Almighty God was upon him. As he reveled in the glory, he felt his defenses come down. The tension of his fear departed and total awe welled up from within and overcame him.

It was then that the Voice of Many Waters called him by name. Startled, and full of fear mixed with peace, Moses responded, "Here I am."

As the dialogue continued, he was fully aware that God Himself had called him out of the ordinary routine of his day. He experienced the presence of God in a way he never thought possible. There was no question, no doubt. His awareness was sensitized as never before. He felt as though every part of him was changed – fully alive.

How could he even think of taking issue with God Himself, yet he was. The words he heard himself speaking were vague, shallow excuses for God's call to him. He knew this was the ultimate paradox of awe and rebellion. It was in this incredible moment that Moses knew his identity would be determined. At issue? God's call to be His servant and a leader of many, or his will to do as he chose. The battleground? His own will.

His excuses were weak, and God met every one of them with response. The decision was his. In an instant it all came flooding back. Those sightless eyes searing his mind. The panic, the disbelief, the depression, the well – oh, that well. Its alluring brokenness. The patterns were too familiar. In a moment he knew it had all started there. The long journey of discovery, learning, deepening, struggling – it all began at the well.

And now, again, the same choices were before him. The tentacles of self-will gripped his heart with the silent shouts of safety, comfort, control. At the same time, the overwhelming energy coming from the glory of this bush seemed to be fueled by the countless, mundane experiences of the past 40 years. Moses knew the decision he made now would be eternal in nature. It was for this climax that he had struggled out of the

hollow of the well and set out on that unknown journey. It was to this moment that all the experiences of
his 40 years of shepherding had pointed.

Overwhelmed with joy and sadness, fear and
confidence, weakness and power, Moses let the tentacles of self-will loose their death grip and fall away.
The powerful presence of God enveloped Moses as he
released himself to become God's servant.

FURTHER READING

Maslow, Abraham, *Toward A Psychology of Being,* Van Nostrand Reinhold, NY, 1968.

McKenna, David L., *Power to Follow Grace to Lead,* Word Publishing, 1989.

Greenleaf, Robert, *Servant Leadership*, Paulist Press, NY, Mahwah, 1977.

Edwards, Gene, *A Tale of Three Kings*, Christian Books, Augusta, ME, 1980.

Foster, Richard, *Prayer: Finding the Heart's True Home*, Harper San Francisco, 1992.

Willard, Dallas, *Spirit of The Disciplines*, Harper San Francisco, 1988.

Hybels, Bill, *Descending Into Greatness,* Zondervan Publishing House, Grand Rapids, MI 1993.

CPSIA information can be obtained at www.ICGtesting.com
Printed in the USA
243240LV00008B/27/A